Diver's Guide
to Florida
and the
Florida Keys

Jim Stachowicz

All charts and drawings
by the author

Windward Publishing, Inc.

105 NE 25th St. P.O. Box 371005 Miami, Fl. 33137

*Special thanks to Mr. Don Pybas of the Florida Sea Grant Program
for information concerning artificial reefs in the state.*

ISBN 0-89317-007-0
Library of Congress No. 76-12928

5 7 9 10 8 6
Printed in the United States of America.

Contents

Foreword

Florida is a water buff's paradise. Every year millions of tourists, and residents, flock to the state's 1800 miles of unparalleled beaches to romp in the clear, calm tropical waters. Boaters are provided with thousands of square miles of tranquil seas and fishermen can enjoy the thrill of fighting some of the finest game-fish in the world.

But Florida's water activities don't stop at the surface. One of the state's greatest attractions is its underwater world which draws tens of thousands of skin divers to its sights from all over — all year long. They can choose from an endless variety of diving sites available throughout the Gulf of Mexico and Atlantic waters, and even deep within the state in crystal clear, fresh-water springs. Out-of-state divers can drive to Florida during their vacations rather than fly to distant parts of the world. They're offered a full range of diving services: air fills, equipment sales and rentals, scuba repair, instruction and guided trips. When they hit the water they can try their hand at spearfishing, underwater photography, collecting marine life, lobstering or shelling. If they simply want to take in the underwater sights, they won't be disappointed.

This typical panorama is part of a coral reef with coral, sponges, sea fans and angelfish obviously displayed. But under cover of the ledges and in the cracks and crevices, a diver would surely discover sea urchins, shell fish or even a spiny lobster.

Topping the list of scenic diving sites is the *only* living coral reef in the country. On this reef, which runs parallel to the Florida Keys, the diver will find a fantasyland of coral forests, brilliantly-colored tropical fish and hundreds of unusual invertebrates. If the diver's interest is shipwrecks, our waters are peppered with them — including 400-year-old Spanish galleons and mammoth World War II freighters.

These underwater attractions are not limited only to certified SCUBA divers. School children, whole families and retired couples are donning mask, snorkel and fins to take in the fascinating underwater spectacles made available by snorkeling. There are excellent diving spots just a few feet off many public beaches. Shallow offshore sites can be reached by hiring guides at coastal motels, hotels and campgrounds, or at dive shops. And just because snorkelers don't dive as deep as scuba divers, it doesn't mean they can't enjoy the same exciting activities.

Nearly anyone interested in "attending" a real-life, natural, unrehearsed underwater spectacular is welcome. The show is packed with action, beauty, humor, color and excitement. A cast of thousands of marine species will dazzle you with bizarre costumes set against a background of incomparable scenery. Come on in anytime — the show is always on.

4

Schooling stripped grunts swarm across the ocean bottom, surprising the unexpecting diver, but also delighting him with their mad-cap frenzy in the tranqui! surroundings.

Elkhorn is one of the most common and expansive corals in the Florida Keys. The diver may find vast forests of this beautiful coral stretching endlessly across the underwater terrain, and often a juvenile French angelfish in its shelter.

Underwater Florida

The main attraction of underwater Florida is the multitude of life that depends on the sea for its survival. Without the flora and fauna, the ocean floor would be a colorless wasteland about as interesting as the surface of the moon. However, the waters surrounding Florida are filled with millions of marine animals ranging in size from microscopic plankton to giant jewfish capable of weighing a half ton. In between, there are thousands of species in every size and description imaginable.

The attention-getters on the reefs are the wildly-colored tropical fish. The majestic angelfish, wafer-thin butterflyfish and multi-hued damselfish are prevalent not only in the Keys but far up the east and west coasts. Members of the large wrasse and parrotfish families sport more colors and patterns than a fabric shop. The tropicals are usually not very skittish and can be easily approached. Breaking up a sea urchin often signals a rare treat for these sea beauties, and after a cautious moment you can have them literally eating out of your hand.

There are so many different species of fish that quite often they are simply named after a distinctive characteristic they possess. A few examples are the needlefish which, of course, is needle-shaped; and the jackknife fish is topped by an unusually long knife-like dorsal fin. The doctorfish and surgeonfish carry a "scalpel" on either side of their tails, the cowfish has small horns, the balloonfish inflates when frightened, the grunts grunt and porcupinefish are covered with pointed spines.

At times, you may swim over a clump of rocks which may appear nearly abandoned of sea life. Closer investigation will often reveal a thriving colony of fish and invertebrates in nearly every hole, crack and crevice. Some species are noted for their ability to blend with their backgrounds. The grouper, triggerfish and doctorfish can actually change color to help them blend with the terrain. The slender trumpetfish suspend themselves vertically to resemble a branch of a sea whip. Camouflage is a great asset in the eat-or-be-eaten nature of the sea.

Schooling fish are a constant part of the underwater scene. Quite often, hundreds of grunt, porgies, spadefish, snapper or baitfish will roam over a reef. The fish find security in swimming in large numbers and often will allow a diver to swim into the school and find himself completely encompassed by fish.

On the living reefs off southern Florida, you'll find dozens of different kinds of beautiful and unusual coral formations. They are created by tiny coral polyps which are permanently affixed to the skeletal remains of their ancestors. Each new generation adds to the growth of the coral structure. Many of these colorful coral growths can be easily identified by an obvious feature or shape. Elkhorn coral resembles the broad antlers of an elk, and staghorn coral looks very much like the pointed antlers of a deer; the same applies to brain, finger, lettuce, pillar and star corals.

Although the fish are the charmers of the reefs, many divers find the "other" marine creatures equally as fascinating. They fall into the enormous group of animals called invertebrates.

You'll see crabs of every size and description darting in and out of cracks and crevices. Brightly-colored sponges cover many areas, some shaped like vases or tubes, others simply growing on rocks in random shapes. The jet-propelled squid may surprise you with an appearance. Sometimes a dozen or more will line up in perfect formation, motionless until you swim too close, signaling a rapid take-off. Transparent jellyfish can be seen pulsating through the water. Sea whips, sea fans and anemones completely cover some bottom areas, swaying with the gentle water currents. Flower-like plume worms will retract as you approach and re-blossom as you retreat. Thousands of other life forms will amaze and intrigue you.

Beautiful tropical fish, colorful coral, fascinating life forms — you'll find them all here — in underwater Florida.

Getting Started in Skin Diving*

For those of you who haven't taken the plunge with a snorkel yet or are interested in becoming a certified diver, the following list of questions most often asked by prospective divers may help to shed some light on the subject.

Snorkel Diving

What is a snorkel diver?

A snorkel diver uses a face mask, snorkel (breathing tube) and swim fins (flippers), observing underwater subjects while floating on the surface of the water. He can dive below the surface by holding his breath.

Is swimming ability essential for snorkeling?

Frankly, you don't even have to know how to swim. Your snorkel gear allows you to float effortlessly on the surface of the water. However, if you ran into trouble, like losing your gear while diving some distance from the beach, *getting back to shore would require extensive swimming skills.*

Is formal training necessary in learning how to snorkel?

If you're content with just hovering around in shallow water, no; but it would be advisable to pick up a book on snorkeling to learn about the proper

---

*The term "skin diving" is defined as underwater diving free of any surface apparatus. The term generally includes both snorkeling and scuba diving.

The brilliantly-colored queen angelfish (distinguished by a bright blue crown) is a common sight among the underwater coral gardens.

A "bouquet" of corals—it includes brain and star corals which are hard corals and the soft corals are a lace gorgonian and a sea fan.

care and use of your equipment. If you prefer, there are snorkeling courses available at some resort areas.

Scuba Diving

What is a scuba diver?

A scuba diver uses the same mask and flippers as the snorkeler but he can breath underwater through a regulator attached to a tank filled with purified compressed air. This will allow him to remain below for about an hour, or submerge to over 100-foot depths.

Is scuba diving safe?

People involved in diver training are proud of the fact that even though the diving population is growing tremendously (over 1 million new scuba divers were trained in the last five years), diving accidents haven't increased proportionally. Accidents most often occur when divers, untrained or newly certified, try to exceed their limits. Extremely few diving fatalities have ever occurred due to equipment failure.

Long trails of air bubbles mark the presence of scuba divers on the bottom of the cavern at Alexander Springs in Ocala National Forest. Small-fry snorkelers watch with interest.

Is training essential?

Yes! Don't ever attempt to teach yourself how to scuba dive. Training courses are available regularly through your YMCA, or a local dive shop or resort that offers certified scuba courses. The course is taught by competent instructors trained by national organizations such as the National Association of Skin Diving Schools (NASDS), the National Association of Underwater Instructors (NAUI), the Professional Association of Diving Instructors (PADI) or the YMCA. These organizations set up their own guidelines for scuba instruction, varying somewhat in procedure but containing the same basic subject matter.

How can I qualify for scuba training?

You must be in good health (some instructors ask for recent health certificates) and be a fairly good swimmer (how good also depends on the individual instructor). You can start as young as 12 years old through a junior scuba course.

What is scuba training like?

After you sign up you'll be put into a class with several other students. Total hours range between 24 to 30 or more, spread out over several weeks and divided into class time, pool training and a couple of open water dives. Some instructors schedule classes at an accelerated pace so that you can be certified before you return home from your vacation. Beginning with classroom sessions, students learn about scuba equipment, first aid, emergency procedures, and the physics of air and water and how it affects a diver's body. Pool training begins with snorkeling procedures and progresses to full scuba practice. Following ample preparation, the student makes a couple of open water dives and receives a certification card upon successful completion.

What are the advantages to owning a certification card?

As a certified scuba diver, you are entitled to buy scuba equipment and air fills, and hire diving guides. In Florida it is becoming increasingly more difficult for non-certified divers to engage in the sport. Your C-card also opens the door to advanced scuba classes.

What kind of advanced scuba courses are available?

A certification card doesn't allow you to dive everywhere under all conditions. It is a *basic* certification, and newly-certified divers should keep well within their limits. To expand your activity there are advanced courses available in deep diving, underwater navigation, limited-visibility diving, light salvage, search and recovery, cave diving, and even in underwater photography and tropical fish collecting. If you'd like to make a career out of diving you can test for "instructor" ratings through one of the national organizations already mentioned.

The spiny lobster of Florida waters is a delicacy similar to the New England lobster except it is all "tail"—it has no claws.

Diving Clubs

Your diving education doesn't stop after you've completed your formal training. As long as you're diving you'll be learning, and one of the best ways to keep on top of things is through a diving club.

In Florida, there are well over a hundred diving clubs varying in size from a few loosely-knit divers to well-organized groups with 50-100 members. Some clubs are developed through places of employment, others are spin-offs from dive shops or are intra-city clubs open to all qualified divers. Whatever the size or type of club, they're the best place for a diver to exchange knowledge and ideas in a sport that is still relatively new.

Perhaps the greatest advantage comes with the ability to dive with a team, which is especially important to scuba diving where buddy diving is always emphasized. When you have the urge to hit the water, you'll probably find a diving buddy from your diving club who is just as eager as you are. Furthermore, your diving costs can be cut substantially. Members of the club can qualify for group rates for instruction, hiring diving guides and travel expenses.

Many club members are not trained scuba divers. In fact, some members may not even be divers. Entire families join the club, with non-diving members planning their own activities around dad's dive with picnicking, camping or just snorkeling in shallow water.

Do you enjoy the thrill of exciting competition? You can test your competence in your own diving specialty with other members of your club, with a neighboring club or in regional and state-wide meets. Contests in underwater photography, spearfishing, marine collecting, underwater navigation and obstacle course trials are only a few examples.

Whether or not you live in Florida, your favorite sport will be safer and more fun if you participate with a club. And if there isn't one in your area, why not start one?

Fresh-Water Diving

Many resident and out-of-state divers may not realize it, but while they're returning home from a south Florida diving vacation, they're probably driving through some of the best spring-diving country in the world.

There are over 100 major springs in north and central Florida with 17 of them rated as first-magnitude. (A first-magnitude spring dispels over 100 cubic feet of water per second.)

The springs are formed by the erosion of the limestone cap that spans under the surface of most of the state. Rainfall is collected underground forming reservoirs and subsurface rivers that eventually cut through the soft stone. Water under pressure is then forced to the surface causing clear springs, rivers or underwater caves.

Divers who have never tried the springs are often puzzled by the enthusiasm shown by the inland divers. A few facts about fresh-water diving will probably clear up the mystery.

- First, you don't need a boat. Most springs and rivers will only be a casual walk from your car.
- Winds and tides are never a factor. You can plan your dive weeks in advance with the assurance that you won't have to cancel due to rough water conditions.
- The crystal-clear spring waters offer unusually high visibilities, often well over 100 feet; and water temperatures don't vary from winter to summer. If a spring was 74°F on the Fourth of July, you can count on it being nearly the same on New Year's Day.

To nearby picnickers and campers, the sight of scuba divers trodding knee-deep through a stream seems almost ludicrous. They're probably not aware of the popularity of fresh-water diving in this state. These divers are wading to the headspring at Blue Springs in Orange City.

Salt water aquarium enthusiasts find an almost unlimited variety of sea life for collecting, even in fresh water springs.

- There are fewer hazards to worry about. You won't find stingrays, moray eels or other hazardous marine life in these waters. Night diving is much safer, too.
- Along with a great variety of fresh-water fish, some spring runs are filled with schools of salt-water fish.
- One of the favorite diving activities here is fossil and artifact hunting. The springs are famous for producing rare and unusual finds.

With all this in its favor, it's not difficult to understand the popularity of fresh-water diving.

Although the boils of many springs can be seen only inches from the surface of the water, others break deep below the ground to form underwater caves and caverns. These narrow shafts are void of light, often silty and can snake through the earth in a labyrinth of multiple channels. Regardless of their conditions, the caves have bred a completely unique diving concept—cave diving.

This increasingly popular form of diving comes with a high potential of danger. But actually, the danger lies within the diver, who is often too eager to experience an exciting adventure. He will test himself against the cave, completely succumbing to the temptation to go farther and explore deeper than his experience permits.

Cave diving can be as safe as any other activity if a common-sense approach is taken. If you can, take a cave diving course. It'll cost you over $100 but it's a small price to pay when you're gambling with your life. Get in touch with the National Association of Cave Diving in Gainesville, Florida, for the name of an instructor near you. There are only a handful of cave diving instructors in the entire world but most make their homes in Florida. If.you can't take a course, dive the less hazardous caves and only with someone with considerable experience. Some of the more popular springs and caves are described in the diving sites section in this book.

13

Weather and Water Conditions

Generally the Sunshine State's weather will be very cooperative for skin diving, allowing good diving conditions the year 'round. Mid-day summer temperatures will average in the high 80's–low 90's throughout the state and only dropping to the mid 70's during south Florida winters, and to the low 60's in the Panhandle area.

Seasonally, the weather runs something like this:

Winter The driest and sunniest time of the year. Winds may vary from the southeast to the northeast with unfavorable winds causing rough seas and turbid water. But you'll find plenty of good diving days and very little rain. Wet suits are necessary in most areas.

Spring Brisk easterly winds are fairly common in early spring but begin to decrease late in the season. Seas begin to calm but rainfall possibilities will increase. Water temperatures are on the rise.

Summer Balmy southeast breezes and excellent water visibilities prevail, but the rainy season is now in full swing. Late afternoon showers and thunderstorms are common so it might be best to plan an early morning dive. Comfortable dives without wet suits are possible on many of the south Florida reefs.

Fall Rainfall decreases and winds increase but not often to the point where they prevent good diving. The likelihood of a hurricane increases in September and October but Florida has been fortunate in recent years in escaping the brunt of a major blow. However, nearby tropical storms and hurricanes may cancel diving trips during this period due to heavy rains and high seas.

Skin diving is a major activity in Florida — and its weather and water are two good reasons why.

Currents

For the most part, Florida divers will find relatively still seas in which to enjoy their diving activities, but there are times when they will encounter fast-moving water within their diving area. Usually the currents will not be flowing fast enough to cancel a dive. Scuba divers learn to swim into a weak current during the first half of the dive and with it on the return back to the boat. If it's too strong, they try another spot. There are many great diving spots along the fringes of the swift Gulf Stream but the stream will occasionally drift over these sites making diving virtually impossible.

Snorkelers will often meet tidal currents when the sea water tries to "squeeze" through narrow entrances to bays, through the inlets to the intra-coastal waterway and in passes between islands and other land masses. A check with the tide tables in the local newspaper will allow you to plan your dive with the slack tide when water motion is at its slowest.

Before you dive, take a minute to check out the spot. You can detect some currents from the surface by a definite discoloration of the water or by floating objects. An anchored boat will also serve as a "weather vane" for current direction.

If you find yourself caught in a swift current while diving, don't try to swim into it. You'll only exhaust yourself in trying to gain ground against the force of tons of water. Some currents will not run very long and you can ride with it or swim perpendicular to it until you reach calmer waters.

Be current conscious.

Night Diving

"It's like nothing I've ever experienced before . . . it's the closest thing to floating in space . . . just a fantastic trip". This was the immediate reaction of a group of scuba divers just returning from their first night dive over Molasses Reef. Diving into a black void doesn't sound very appealing to many divers but enthusiastic descriptions like these are waking day-trippers to the uniqueness of sunless plunges.

Reefs take on a whole new look after sundown. Nocturnal sea life, hidden during the day, can be caught "au naturel" at night as they leave their lairs to feed. Fish you don't see over a reef during daylight will surprise you by their presence at night. Coral polyps withdraw from the sun but blossom at night to catch floating particles of food. Sleeping fish you can hold in your hand, colors like you've never seen underwater before — your favorite dive spot takes on an entirely different look.

Needless to say, extra precautions should be taken by everyone partici-pating in a night dive. Buddy diving should be more emphasized than usual; the group should be kept closer to the boat and to each other — this also applies to snorkel diving. At least one underwater light per person, tied to the wrist, is a minimum requirement. Novice scuba divers should wait until they've chalked up a few more daytime dives and feel more relaxed in the water before attempting a night dive.

Night diving is becoming very popular with many divers, and when prop-erly planned and sensibly approached it can be a safe and enjoyable change-of-pace activity.

Photo courtesy Florida Department of Commerce

These divers are about to explore an underwater cave in north-central Florida. Their next dive may be over a shipwreck off Jacksonville for spearfishing or out of Key Largo to photograph the blazing colors of a coral reef. Florida diving offers something for everyone.

Florida Diving Activities

The following are brief descriptions of the most popular diving activities you can enjoy in Florida waters.

Spearfishing

For many divers, the greatest underwater thrill comes with hunting and spearing a tasty food fish for the dinner table. Rarely is the Florida spearfisherman deprived of this exciting thrill — providing he knows where to go and how to go about it.

Florida waters abound with exceptional opportunities for the underwater hunter. From Jacksonville, south to the Keys and all the way up the Gulf coast, there are dozens of sites teeming with large fish valued for their delicious taste. The sites where the "big ones" can be found are located around natural and artificial reefs in deep water, ledges near the Gulf Stream, and around large sunken ships. These areas provide a base for tiny plant and animal life which attract small bait fish which, in turn, attract larger fish. They also provide hiding places for many of the fish. In the clear waters of Florida, you can detect inshore reefs from your boat by looking for dark patches in the water or buoys set up by local divers. However, easily accessible inshore reefs and wrecks are apt to be cleaned out of good spearing game.

The spearfisherman has a distinct advantage over the surface angler, primarily because he can sight his fish underwater. But the technique of spearing a prize fish requires skills comparable to those of a hunter stalking prey on land. First he must find worthy game. Many fish have the ability to camouflage themselves or hide in the bottom terrain before a diver can sight it. Once the fish is sighted, the diver must maneuver close enough to penetrate it with the spear. Some spear guns are limited to less than ten feet in range, and it's amazing how often your quarry will remain just outside of spearing distance.

There are a great variety of spear guns on the market, but the top choices of most Florida divers are the type powered by a series of rubber slings. The medium sized rubber gun will be adequate for most of the fish you'll see. It measures over four feet long and carries about a three foot shaft attached to a strong nylon line and fired by a trigger mechanism. Several types of spearheads are available depending on your particular kind of hunting.

If you want to add more sport to the hunt, try a Hawaiian sling; but don't be disappointed with your initial results. The use of this kind of spear requires considerable skill and a little bit of muscle.

The sling is a much simpler spearing device than the trigger guns. A five-foot shaft slides into a short piece of tubing to which is attached a rubber sling. Holding the tube and drawing on the sling fires the shaft. There is no line so the diver must follow the fish after it's hit. The Hawaiian sling is best for smaller prey.

There has been quite a bit of controversy concerning the flagrant use of spearguns by many unconcerned divers. Complaints arise about spearfishermen shooting anything and everything they see, then leaving dozens of fish on the beach to spoil. Others use the gun so carelessly as to endanger bathers or their own diving buddies. Fortunately, most spearfishermen treat a speargun like they would any other dangerous weapon and are very selective in what they shoot, spearing only what they intend to filet.

These are a few of the many great food fish sought by the Florida spearfisherman:

Hogfish or *Hogsnapper*   This is one of the best tasting fish in Florida, and, of course, one of the most hunted. They have a distinctive shape and are easily recognized. The average size is 4-5 pounds but 20 pounders have been taken.

Grouper   There are several worthy members in this family. Two of them are the Nassau grouper and the black grouper. They both average about 10 pounds but can reach over 50. Other groupers include the red, the Warsaw and the rock hind. All groupers are very fond of ledges and caves.

Snappers The most popular and the largest snapper is the red snapper. Forty-pounders have been speared but they generally average less than 10 pounds. Other favorite snappers are the mangrove, the schoolmaster and the mutton snapper, all averaging a couple of pounds.

Sheepshead These fish are often seen schooling in great numbers. They average less than 5 pounds but can exceed 15 lbs.

Tropical Fish Collecting

Most divers are forced to limit their activities to weekends or vacations, but many divers are finding they can extend their "down time" by getting involved in the fascinating hobby of marine collecting and aquarium-keeping. They enjoy the challenge of collecting marine species while diving and later they can spend hours studying the habits of sea life from a salt-water aquarium. At the same time the aquarium adds an attractive conversation piece to the home.

Marine species collecting is enjoyed by both snorkelers and scuba divers. Specimens can be found around close inshore rock formations just off the beach as well as on deep offshore ledges many miles from shore. Equipment needs aren't elaborate—snorkelers have come up with beautiful tropical fish simply by using a special hand net sold at most local dive shops. Some divers prefer to use slurp guns—clear plexiglas cylinders with a piston attached to a handle. Drawing on the handle will force water and nearby tropicals into the barrel. The captured fish is then transferred to a plastic milk carton attached by line to the diver or a bucket floating on the surface. (Deep water species must be decompressed when brought to the surface to allow for the change in water pressure.) When the catch is finally brought to the boat, it is transferred again to a plastic or styrofoam holding container for the ride back home. If the fish are to be left in the container for an hour or more, they should be supplied with oxygen through a battery-operated air pump and air stone. If you live out-of-state, check with an aquarium shop for proper packing and shipping procedures for tropical fish.

There was a time when maintaining salt-water specimens in a contained environment was practiced only by highly-trained marine biologists. Fresh-water aquarists who tried to switch over to a marine tank usually lost their specimens in a few days. Today, through the development of efficient filtration devices, all-glass tanks, synthetic salt-water mixes, advanced medications, new frozen foods and publications on the latest techniques, the marine aquarist can enjoy a trouble-free tank for many years.

The Atlantic and Gulf waters of Florida offer the collector a wide variety of beautiful tropical fish and unusual invertebrates. A few of the more popular species are listed.

Damselfish This very large family includes the sergeant major, beau gregory, blue chromis, yellowtail damsel and the bi-color damsel. They are colorful, very common in Florida and excellent fish for the beginning aquarist. Damselfish are hardy but tend to be aggressive in a tank, especially to their own kind.

Angelfish   All angelfish species are very popular aquarium fish. They are very colorful, especially in their juvenile stage. Included in this family are the rock beauty, queen, blue, gray, french and pygmy angelfish.

Butterflyfish   The longnose, banded and foureye butterflyfish are a few of the most sought-after tropicals in Florida but they are rarer on the reefs than the angelfish. Some specimens are very fussy eaters, feeding only on live food and only when they are in the mood.

Wrasses   These are very numerous, hardy and colorful fish that do well in aquariums except for their peculiar habit of burying themselves under the gravel at night. An aquarium can look lifeless during the evening hours if it contains only wrasses.

Other favorite aquarium fish include the neon goby, cubbyu, tangs and hamlets. Invertebrates do well in aquariums, and some collectors keep *only* invertebrates.

Underwater Photography

Ever since a Frenchman took the first known underwater picture over 80 years ago, man has been fascinated by the prospect of underwater photography. But it wasn't until scuba diving became popular in the 50's that divers, excited by their underwater discoveries, begged for underwater cameras and camera housings that would help them to capture their findings on film.

Today, the amateur underwater photographer has a wide choice of photographic equipment available to him—from inexpensive plexiglas housings for simpler cameras to complete photographic systems including flash and strobe units, assorted lenses, filters and light meters. Color movies are also possible through well-designed housings. Underwater photographers are enjoying more flexibility than ever before.

Many divers aren't terribly concerned with top quality pictures and prefer to use the same simple non-adjustable camera they use for those family shots at home. Divers who are a little more particular and desire more latitude in their photography prefer the 35mm camera. Whatever your choice, anyone taking a camera underwater should be aware of the vast differences in shooting in a wet environment. Refraction, light loss and color loss are some of the factors they must deal with.

Refraction is the bending of light rays through water, glass or air. In the divers case, the light passes from the water through his face mask which makes objects appear about 25% closer than they actually are. If you hold your arm straight out in the water you'll notice it looks considerably shorter. Refraction isn't a great problem for the photographer. If he has an adjustable focus on his camera he simply sets it to the apparent distance. The camera will "see" the subject at the same distance as the photographer.

Light loss. As soon as you take your camera underwater you lose a certain amount of the light you had while you were above the water. This can be caused by reflection of light off the surface of the water, surface action, depth of the water, or suspended particles in the water. Any one or a combination of these factors can considerably reduce the light you have to work with. If you are shooting underwater pictures with little sunlight in rough, turbid water at 100 feet, don't count on great shots. If you are in clear, calm, shallow water with an overhead sun you have about as much light as if you were working above water with a hazy sun. To compensate for considerable light loss, underwater photographers can use high speed films or artificial light.

Color loss. There's a myriad of colors to be found beneath the sea but you won't see them in deep water. The more water you put between you and the sun, the fewer colors you'll have in your pictures. The warm colors are the first to go, beginning with red, followed by orange and yellow. At about 80 feet, everything takes on a blue or green shade. To keep a wide spectrum of colors in your shots, shoot in shallow water or use a flash or strobe at color-robbing depths.

PHOTO TIP: Many beginning underwater photographers have a tendency to shoot down on a subject which usually results in flat and uninteresting pictures. Try to shoot at an upward angle to your subject for a change. Your pictures will be more dramatic and contain more contrast.

A special note: It's very easy to get totally involved in photographing the hundreds of possible subjects around you. Don't over-extend yourself beyond your diving limits to get that extra special shot.

Lobstering

The first of August is an unusual day in Florida. On that day many employers ponder over a sharp increase in absenteeism, coastal motels are filled to capacity and fishermen notice considerably more empty boats on the water flying the familiar diver-down flag. The explanation is quite simple—Florida's lobster season has opened.

Some divers call them "spinies", to others they are "crawfish" or "bugs", but whatever you call them the Florida Spiny Lobster is the cause for all the lobster fever.

If you sight one of these crustaceans, you'll know it; their appearance is unmistakable. The shell is orange-brown and white and covered with tiny, forward-pointing spines which gives this lobster its name. The two long antennae which are used as feelers are followed by the carapace or upper shell, then a wide hinged tail. Other appendages include five pairs of long, skinny legs and smaller antennae and arms. Unlike many other species the spiny lobster has no claws. Generally, they average a few pounds in weight and measure about a foot long but big 12- to 14-pounders have been picked up by divers.

The spiny lobster can be found off most Florida coastal areas, from close inshore reefs to deep-water ledges, under rocks, in crevices or any kind of hole large enough to accommodate them and offer them protection from their enemies. Sometimes only the antennae can be seen waving outside the shelter.

All you need for bug collecting is a good pair of gloves, a prodder or "tickling stick", a meshed holding bag and some fast reflexes. The animal is near sighted but extremely quick.

Catching techniques vary. Some divers find that if they can keep the antennae busy by touching one lightly with a hand and the other with their face mask, they can grab the lobster with the free hand. Others use the prodder to reach into the hole and tap the spiny on the tail forcing the lobster to jump forward, out of its home. If the spiny is already partly out of its hole when you sight it, you may be able to snatch it from above and wiggle it free (the spines and appendages will cling to the inside of the hole). If you try to grab the antennae they will probably break off in your hand unless you can pull without bending them. Remember, moray eels also like dark places and will occasionally share a lair with a lobster.

When you've finally brought home your limit, boil the tails (only) in salted water for about 15 minutes and serve with melted butter.

There are several laws governing the taking of the crawfish. Refer to the diving laws article for specifics.

Shelling

For centuries, the shell-collector was a beachcomber who patiently scoured the sand, hoping to find an interesting specimen in reasonably good shape. With the advent of scuba diving, a whole new way of shelling came of age. Many skin divers found they could dive far offshore in deep water and find rarer, live mollusks bearing perfect shells. Even snorkelers have found many beauties just a few feet off the beach. Skin divers don't have to settle for broken, sun-bleached specimens. Today, many divers are turning to shell-collecting as their only underwater activity.

There is excellent shelling to be found along all of Florida's coastline, especially in the waters off the Keys and the west coast. The tranquil seas of the Gulf of Mexico afford some of the best shelling in the country. Sanibel Island, west of Ft. Myers, has a shelling reputation known throughout the world. Other excellent areas can be found from Marco Island all the way up to the Panhandle. In the Keys, the shallow waters of Florida Bay are perfect for shelling. This is conch country, with some specimens of Horse Conch growing to over two feet in length. The east coast is not without excellent shelling spots and divers here have also brought up some rare and beautiful specimens.

Many shells, like the conchs, can be seen completely exposed on the surface of the sand but covered with a layer of marine growth as camouflage. Other shells, like the cowries, can be found attached to the undersides of rocks. If you are looking for olives, follow the snaking trails in the sand. There's a good chance you'll find that mollusk at the end of it.

Diving for shells is an absorbing activity which is attracting more and more divers. If shelling is your game—Florida is your place.

Florida Diving Sites

The charts and site descriptions on the following pages will be helpful to you in planning your dive. They represent the best diving locations offered in every part of the state. Some sites will offer excellent snorkeling, others are best for novice scuba divers and still others are for the advanced scuba diver. Don't attempt the advanced sites unless you're thoroughly qualified.

The charts are not intended for use as navigational aids and depths and distances indicated are approximate. If you aren't familiar with the waters you intend to dive, hire a guide. You can usually find them at dive shops in every region of the state. A trip will cost from $10-20 but you'll save yourself a lot of time in finding a site. If you're interested in a close inshore spot you can rent a boat from a marina.

If your local dive shop doesn't offer guided trips, they may be able to help you make arrangements to go out with a nearby diving club.

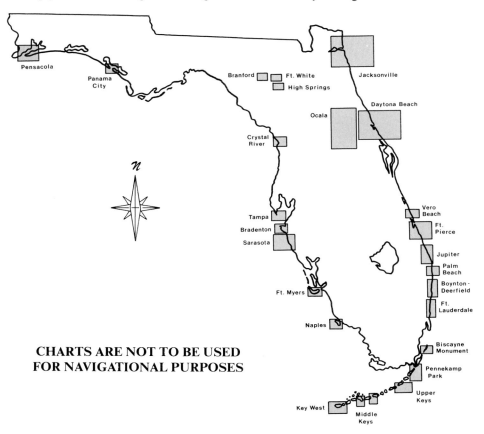

CHARTS ARE NOT TO BE USED FOR NAVIGATIONAL PURPOSES

Jacksonville

It's a long trip, about 31 miles, but few divers ever complain after a dive on the *Casa Blanca*. The 285-foot Navy LST was intentionally sunk to serve as an artificial reef for sportsmen in the Jacksonville area. It's a deep wreck, still intact, lying in a little over 100 feet of water, with the top structure beginning at 55 feet. After you swim through tons of baitfish, you'll see many snapper, spadefish, lots of barracuda, grouper and jewfish up to 600 pounds.

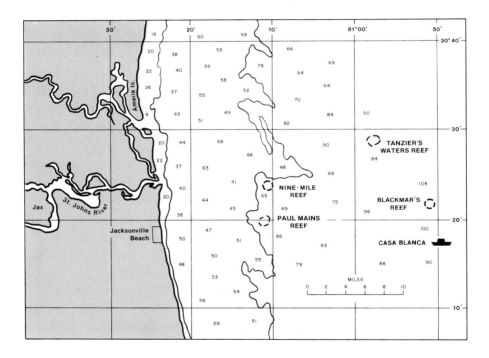

If you really want to make a day of it, less than five miles NNW of the *Casa Blanca* is Blackmar's Reef. This is an artificial reef made up of barges, tugs, and a ferry, and harbors many of the same fish species as the LST. This dive is a deeper dive, averaging about 110 feet. Farther north is Tanzier's Waters Reef in depths of about 90 feet. These deep water sites are recommended for seasoned divers only.

A lot closer to shore lie Nine-Mile Reef and Paul Mains Reef. Like the reefs previously mentioned, they are also composed of barges, tugs and assorted material. These closer reefs are in approximately 60 to 70 feet of water.

23

Daytona Beach

Out of the Ponce de Leon Inlet, south of Daytona Beach, you can gain access to a series of offshore reefs. About 20 miles ENE of the inlet lies the Party Grounds Reef, 22 miles due east is East Eleven Reef and it's over 28 miles SE to Ten Fathoms Reef. They all bear a plateau shape with depths averaging between 65-85 feet.

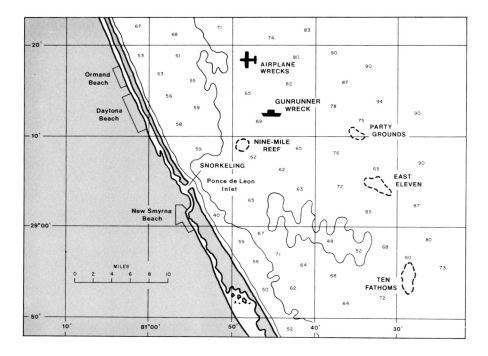

Along the 10-15 foot ledges you'll find many good spearing fish. Red snapper to 40 lbs. have been seen. Heavy hogfish, black and Nassau grouper and slews of sheepshead are common. Lobster come pretty big — up to 12 lbs.

The reefs do not offer exceptional photographic opportunities but tropical fish collectors and shellers can be kept busy on them.

For a closer dive site, try the artificial Nine-Mile Reef. It's a large collection of cars, a barge and assorted rubble in 70 feet of water.

Before the turn of the century, a steam ship was sunk 14 miles NE of the inlet while involved in gun running during the Spanish-American War. Today she is a lure to thousands of fish, including mammoth jewfish. For a nice change-of-pace dive, try the airplane wreckage about 12 miles east of Ormond Beach.

Vero Beach

Most of the diving action around the Vero Beach area occurs relatively close to shore. Divers can choose from a shipwreck, an airplane wreck or off-the-beach rock formations.

The wreckage of the *Breckonshire* lies in 15-20 feet of water about 200 yards off the Holiday Inn. The ship's boiler breaks the surface of the water making it possible to sight it from the beach. Along with tropical angelfish and highhats you'll see snappers, sheepshead and an occasional small grouper.

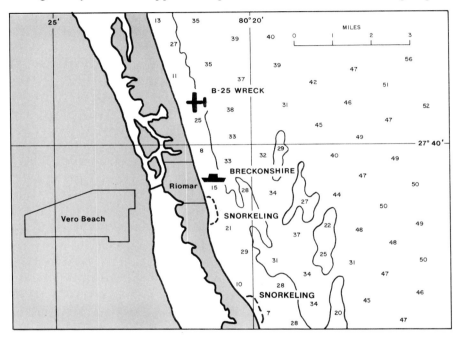

During WWII, Vero Beach was the site of a busy flight training base. Several planes have crashed in the nearby seas, including a B-25 about two miles north of Vero, 300 yards off shore in 20-25 foot depths. Another plane, (not shown on chart) is about nine miles south of the city, half a mile offshore in 15-18 feet of water.

Areas popular with snorkelers are found at the south end of Humiston Public Beach and farther south near Round Island. The reefs are 100 to 200 feet offshore.

Fort Pierce

There are two interesting wreck sites off Fort Pierce. Each one offers its own particular type of diving but they both have something in common: they were torpedoed less than one day apart, probably by the same German U-boat.

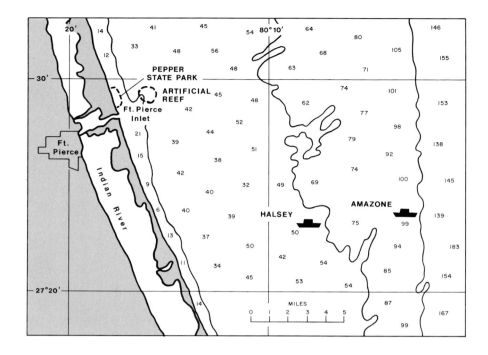

The closer wreck, the *Halsey,* is a large tanker sunk on May 6th, 1942, and now lies in 50 feet of water about 12 miles SE of the Fort Pierce Inlet. It's the larger of the two wrecks and a more impressive site than the other.

The farther wreck is the freighter *Amazone,* torpedoed on May 7th, 1942, about 16 miles ESE of the inlet. It's broken up in three parts in about 100 feet of water. Spearfishing is better on this wreck, with "herds" of grouper and snapper about.

Getting closer to shore, snorkelers are offered a good spot off Pepper Park, just north of the inlet. This site is a preserved area and no spearfishing is allowed. Somewhere in this vicinity, a skin diver found thousands in coins from a ship carrying a U.S. Army payroll.

Jupiter

Between Stuart and Jupiter there are several fine inshore spots well worth consideration.

About six miles south of the St. Lucie Inlet and less than a mile offshore lies the Peck Lake Reef. It's a conglomeration of huge boulders, caves and ledges starting at about 15 feet and dropping down to 30. If you don't like diving with a crowd, you'd better skip this spot during lobster season.

Five miles north of the Jupiter Inlet lies the *Gulf Pride* wreck, or at least what's left of it. Its bow section is less than a mile offshore in 40 feet of water. Spearfishermen have taken some big red snapper and sheepshead here.

26

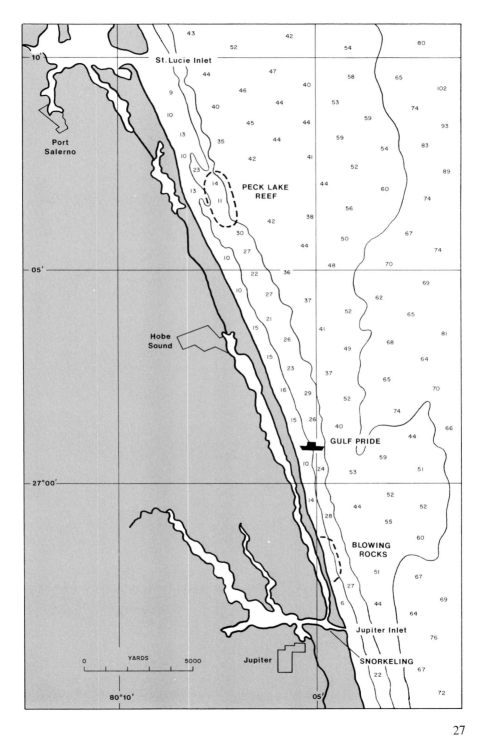

Travel three miles south of the wreck and you are at the Blowing Rocks, a spotty inshore reef accessible from the beach. Snorkelers will see tropicals, schooling fish and many crustaceans.

A great spot for junior skin divers is at the Du Bois Park on the Jupiter Inlet. Between the large rocks bordering the inlet on the south side there's a calm pool safe enough for tots and close enough to open water to attract many types of fish. Parrotfish, porkfish, damsels and a few angelfish are usually around.

Palm Beach

A triple treat awaits divers who venture out to the wrecks one mile NE of the Palm Beach Inlet. Three ships, the *PC1170,* the *Amarylis* and the *Mizpah,* were intentionally sunk very close to each other to form an artificial reef that rates as one of the best diving spots on the east coast. The reef is a protected area and spearfishing is not allowed.

The most dramatic of the three is the 165-foot patrol boat, *Mizpah.* It sits in 80 feet of water with the superstructure beginning at 50 feet. Several open hatchways allow entrance into the craft where you'll often find large schools of grunt. (An underwater light is useful for exploring inside.) The wreck is congested with sea life: large tropical fish, jacks, schools of barracuda, big turtles and moray eels. Strong currents are common until you snuggle close to the wrecks. Novice divers would be more comfortable at the Breakers Reef.

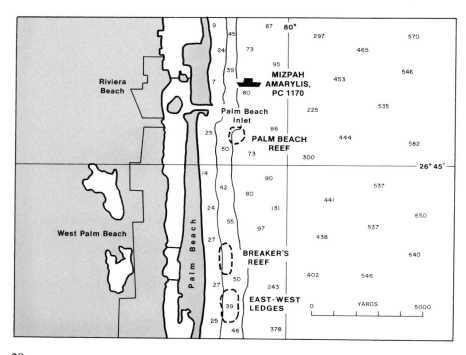

The Breakers is one of the most colorful reefs to be found so close to shore. It's less than a mile east of the famous Breakers Hotel, and four miles south of the Palm Beach Inlet. Finger and flower coral, gorgonians, sea fans and sponges are found on large rock formations in 50-60 feet of water. 10-12 foot ledges are loaded with sea life. Small tropicals, lots of rock beauties, and schooling porkfish and spadefish are everywhere.

Curiosity seekers must check out the Palm Beach Reef. In addition to containing several traditional shipwrecks, it's the permanent parking place for a once perfectly good Rolls Royce.

Another popular site is the East-West Ledges just south of the Breakers Reef.

Boynton Beach to Deerfield Beach

Within this 20-mile stretch, the snorkeler and scuba diver have many excellent diving sites — and all within a mile from shore.

The snorkeling sites are rock formations which can be easily detected from the beach as dark blue patches on the water. The rocks provide a haven for hundreds of fish species. Schooling porgies, doctorfish, grunts, and wrasses are very common. Parrotfish, snappers, angelfish, and damselfish are always a part of the scene along with coronetfish, balloonfish, triggerfish, squids and even octopuses. Tropical fish collecting along these inshore reefs is excellent. Occasionally, heavy seas will cover the rocks with sand which will force most of the marine life away. Another heavy blow might expose the reef again and once more it's teeming with fish. If your once-favorite spot is now covered, don't give up on it, try it again another day.

The offshore reefs at Boynton, Delray and Highland beaches are about ¾ mile out and one to two miles long. The seaward side of the reef slopes down to nearly 100 feet and the inside ledges drop straight down from 50 to 65 feet. Some of these walls are nearly 20 feet high. Living coral, sea fans, anemones and sponges flourish on the reefs. Tiny tropicals to big jacks and grouper are always seen. Spearfishermen, underwater photographers and collectors are rarely disappointed.

The Delray Wreck is a very popular site where many diving instructors hold their student qualifying dives. It's about 100 yards off the south end of Delray Public Beach. The ship is broken in two parts 20 feet down with the boiler only inches from the surface. Many large tropicals, schools of baitfish and barracuda frequent the site. Boatless scuba divers often swim to the wreck from the beach with compasses to direct them back.

The Boca Patch is a flat reef but it's loaded with tropicals, sea fans, sponges and tiny plume worms. It's a paradise for the micro-photographer who will find a crazy-quilt of colors and unusual subjects. The reef is just south of the Boca Raton Inlet and about 500 yards offshore. Depths average about 35-40 feet.

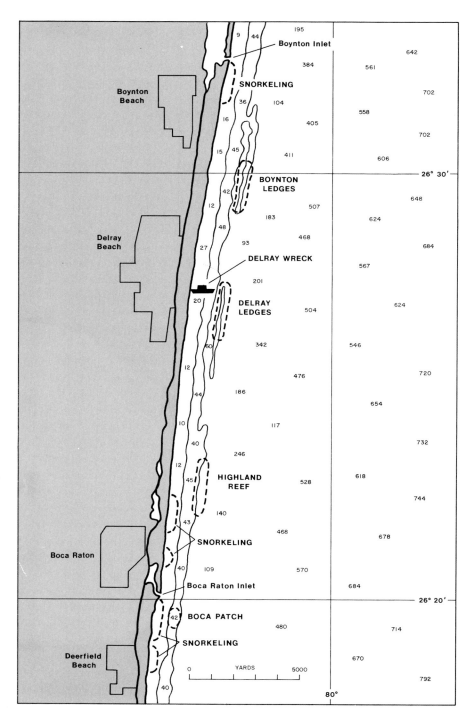

Boynton Inlet

SNORKELING

Boynton Beach

BOYNTON LEDGES

Delray Beach

DELRAY WRECK

DELRAY LEDGES

HIGHLAND REEF

SNORKELING

Boca Raton

Boca Raton Inlet

BOCA PATCH

SNORKELING

Deerfield Beach

26° 30'

26° 20'

80°

YARDS

0   5000

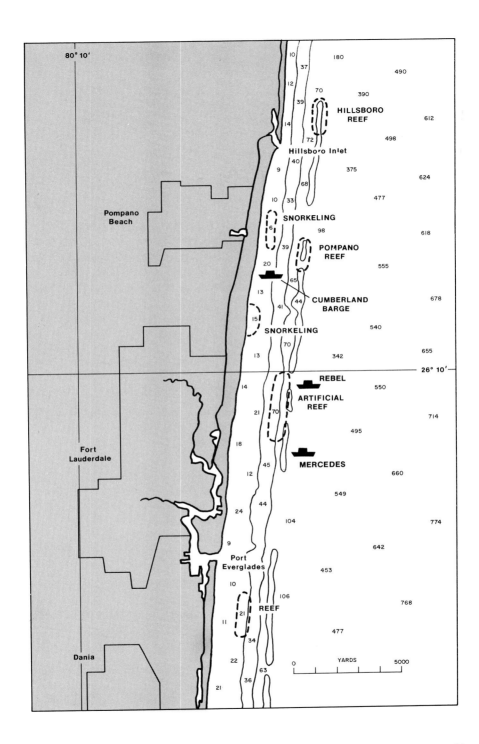

80° 10'

180
490
37
12
39
70
390
HILLSBORO
REEF
612
14
72
498
Hillsboro Inlet
40
9
375
68
624
10
33
477
Pompano
Beach
6
SNORKELING
98
618
39
POMPANO
REEF
20
555
65
13
41
CUMBERLAND
BARGE
678
15
SNORKELING
540
70
13
342
655

26° 10'

14
REBEL
550
21
70
ARTIFICIAL
REEF
714
18
495
45
MERCEDES
660
12
549
44
24
104
774
9
642
Port
Everglades
453
10
106
768
21
REEF
11
477
34
Dania
22
63
YARDS
0   5000
36
21

Fort
Lauderdale

31

Fort Lauderdale

The Hillsboro and Pompano reefs are very similar to the reefs between Boynton and Deerfield beaches. They have the same types of sea life, they're about the same distance from shore and in approximately the same depths. The Hillsboro reef is the more popular because of its proximity to the inlet.

Between the two piers and about a half mile offshore rests the *Cumberland*, an old ammunition barge now broken up on the shelf of the first reef. Twenty foot depths make this site a good novice dive.

Further south, centered between Sunrise Blvd. and Oakland Park Blvd. lies a huge artificial reef about a mile off the coast. It contains several scuttled ships, thousands of tires and large cement arrow jacks. It's a magnet for all types of fish, including snapper, hogfish and schooling grunts and spadefish.

Two large shipwrecks are fairly recent additions to Ft. Lauderdale diving. Both were intentionally sunk in 1985. The *Rebel* is a 150 foot freighter resting in 100+ feet of water. The 200 foot freighter *Mercedes* is about a mile farther south. You may recall, the ship blew ashore during a storm at Palm Beach and was fast aground. After several months of effort the freighter was finally pulled free, towed to a location off Fort Lauderdale and sunk in 90 feet of water.

Other shipwrecks in this vicinity include the *Houseboard* and the *Monomy*.

One and a half miles off Hollywood are 3 sections of the Tenneco oil drilling platforms. Average depths are about 100 feet. (Not shown on map.)

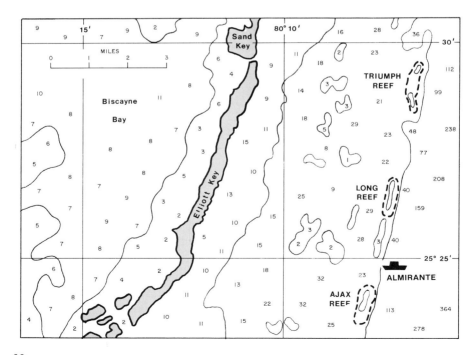

Miami

Just within the last 10 years, the waters off Miami have become filled with one of the largest concentrations of shipwrecks in the country. Many are too deep for sport diving, but several are well within safe diving limits.

Southeast of Key Biscayne is the very popular *Biscayne* wreck. In the same general vicinity is the freighter *Proteus,* the *Arida,* the Woolworth yacht *South Seas,* the *Orion* and the *Ultra Freeze.* Depths range from 55 to 120 feet. Farther south is the freighter *Blue Fire* (off Soldier Key) and the *Almirante* (five miles off Elliott Key).

Several excellent coral reefs are located within the boundaries of the Biscayne National Monument only 15 miles south of Miami. Triumph, Long and Ajax Reefs are among the most popular. All three reefs are less than five miles from Elliott Key in depths averaging 15-20 feet, gently sloping to 60 feet on the seaward side. The reefs are thick with tropicals, hard and soft corals and sponges. The marine life in the national monument is similar to that found in the John Pennekamp State Park, and like the state park, these reefs are protected from collecting of any kind. All the old shipwrecks in the area must also be left undisturbed.

John Pennekamp Coral Reef State Park

The unique underwater park is a state preserve area extending over 20 miles parallel to the upper keys and stretching out to sea for five to six miles. It encompasses nearly 100 square miles of the only living reef in the country. Here you'll find over 40 different varieties of live coral, hundreds of beautiful tropical fish species and a fantasyland of unusual sponges, sea fans and sea whips.

The park has been protected since 1960 from coral collectors, fish collectors, and spearfishermen. In fact, the only thing you can take in the park is pictures. If you're an underwater photographer, you'll never run out of subjects on the coral reefs.

Grecian Rocks

About seven miles east of the mouth of South Sound Creek is one of the best snorkeling areas in the park. Grecian Rocks is a 500-yard shallow water reef where snorkelers can study micro sea life only inches from their mask and underwater photographers can snap beautiful color shots without the use of artificial light. Scores of brilliantly colored tropical fish species swarm over large fields of shallow-water coral.

During rough seas, the protected western side of Grecian Rocks is one of the few diveable spots in the Keys.

Christ of the Deep

Less than one mile NNE of Grecian Rocks stands the nine-foot bronze "Christ of the Deep" statue. The unusual two-ton figure with arms outstretched towards the surface is set in 20 feet of water near Key Largo Dry Rocks.

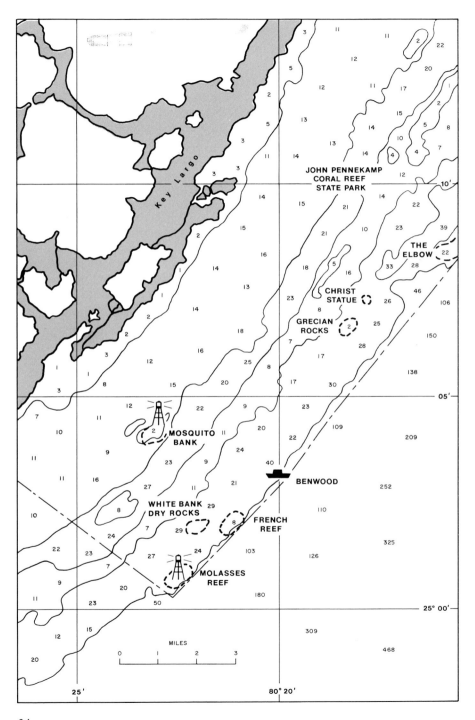

JOHN PENNEKAMP
CORAL REEF
STATE PARK

THE
ELBOW

CHRIST
STATUE

GRECIAN
ROCKS

Key Largo

BENWOOD

MOSQUITO
BANK

WHITE BANK
DRY ROCKS

FRENCH
REEF

MOLASSES
REEF

MILES

0   1   2   3

10'

05'

25° 00'

80° 20'

25'

34

The statue lies in a beautiful setting with many dramatic coral formations nearby. It makes an interesting and unusual photographic subject.

Molasses Reef

Molasses is one of the finest coral reefs in the state. Its endless beauty will continue to hypnotize a diver regardless of the number of times he dives it. The terrain of the reef varies from sloping hills and valleys to plunging coral cliffs providing dramatic underwater passes. Every inch of the reef is alive with coral, gorgonians, tropicals and even large game fish. The site is an underwater photographer's heaven.

Molasses is about seven miles SE of Key Largo and is topped with a 50 foot light tower making it easy to locate, day or night.

French Reef

Two miles NE of Molasses Reef lies French reef. It's deeper than Molasses and is noted for its coral caves and arches, almost resembling structures from a past civilization. Try it on your way to the *Benwood* wreck.

M.V. Benwood

The wreck of the *Benwood* must be one of the most visited shipwrecks in the world. The 300-foot freighter lies within the boundaries of the state park and is usually on the schedule of most diving guides operating out of Key Largo. It's about four miles NE of Molasses Reef or 1½ miles from French Reef.

The ship was built in England in 1910 and survived for the next 32 years until it was struck by a triple disaster in 1942. During the peak of German U-boat activity along the Florida Coast, the *Benwood* was sighted and torpedoed by a German submarine. As it tried to limp back to port, it was accidentally rammed by a friendly ship, then her own shells exploded amidship sending her to the bottom in 30-50 feet of water.

Other fine diving sites within the park are The Elbow, Mosquito Bank, White Bank Dry Rocks, and the *City of Washington* wreck.

Upper Keys

One of the largest and most impressive sights in these waters is the wreck of the *Eagle*. The freighter was intentionally sunk in 1985 about 5 miles offshore in 100 feet of water. It's a must dive for more experienced divers.

About five miles off Plantation Key are several fine reefs, fairly close together, which offer something for every type of diver.

Little Conch Reef is a great spot for snorkeling and novice scuba with depths ranging from 10 to 25 feet. Impressive forests of elkhorn coral and giant pillar coral make this reef popular with photographers. Little Conch is also the site of the Spanish galleon, *El Infante,* one of the largest treasure ships

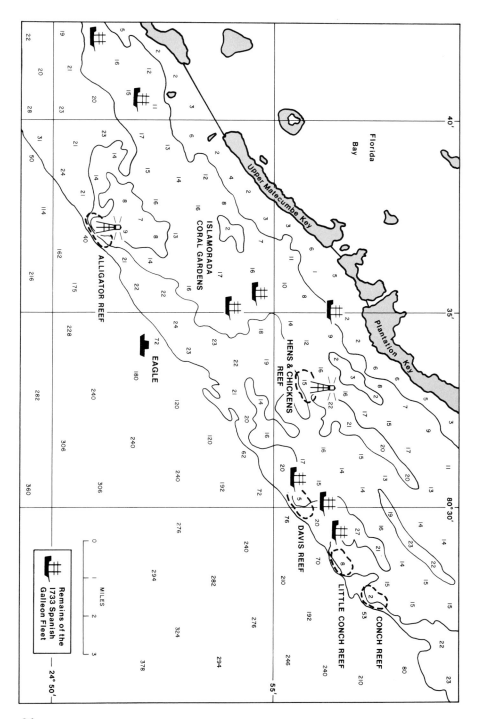

Remains of the
1733 Spanish
Galleon Fleet

MILES
0 1 2 3

Florida
Bay

Upper Matecumbe Key

Plantation Key

ISLAMORADA
CORAL GARDENS

ALLIGATOR REEF

EAGLE

HENS & CHICKENS
REEF

DAVIS REEF

LITTLE CONCH REEF

CONCH REEF

40'

35'

80°30'

55'

24° 50'

of the 1733 fleet. Tropical fish collectors and shellers are always finding excellent specimens here.

Conch Reef is a deeper reef. It lies on the fringes of the Gulf Stream where its seaward side slopes down to nearly 100 feet. Spearfishing is legal out here and many large fish are available.

Davis Reef is two miles SW of Conch Reef. An interesting coral ledge spans for several hundred feet on the inside of the reef where you'll see massive schools of grunt, anglefish, parrotfish and an occasional moray eel. Depths average about 30 feet.

Alligator Reef is about four miles SE from the southern end of Upper Matecumbe Key. Its location is marked by a 100-foot high light tower. It was named for the man-of-war, U.S.S. *Alligator*, which was used to suppress pirating along the Keys. It sank in 1822 and lies a few hundred feet SE of the tower.

On your way back from the outer reefs you may want to check out the Islamorada Coral Gardens, Hens and Chickens Reef or one of the galleon sites.

Middle Keys

Marathon is the center for diving services in the middle keys. Less than five miles offshore lies the notable Sombrero Key which is pinpointed by the 150-foot light tower atop it. Sombrero is a pretty reef that both snorkelers and scuba divers can enjoy. Depths start only inches from the surface and drop to 50-60 feet on the outside. Photographers and sightseers will be intrigued with the area but there aren't many spearing fish around. Large schools of barracuda occasionally drift by though, creating a little excitement among the divers. Sombrero Key is also an excellent night diving spot.

Delta Shoals is located about a mile and a half from Sombrero Key. At the edge of the shoal nearly a dozen coral ridges start to trail out to sea in 10 feet of water and taper off in about 20-foot depths. Several ships have been caught by the ridges. Their locations can be detected by the presence of ballast rock and miscellaneous rubble between the coral formations.

East Washerwoman Shoal is also marked by a tower. It's a good spot for snorkelers who will find many varieties of shallow-water coral and plenty of gorgonians. The shoal is only a couple of miles from shore.

Roughly 6-7 miles SSW of Big Pine Key you'll find Looe Key, considered by many to be one of the best coral reefs in the Keys. It was named after the British frigate H.M.S. *Looe* which struck the reef in 1744. Looe has a series of finger-like coral formations which allows the snorkeler to work in shallow water and the scuba diver to descend alongside 20-30 foot ledges. The seaward side of the reef drops off to 100 feet where larger fish can be seen. Looe Key is a national marine sanctuary and spearfishing is not allowed.

Also take a look at Big Pine Shoal—it's topped with a light and easy to find.

A fairly recent and exciting addition to middle keys diving is the *Thunderbolt* wreck. You'll find it southeast of Marathon, in over 100 feet of water on the edge of the Gulf Stream.

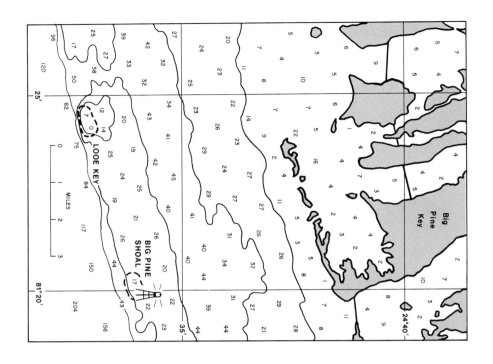

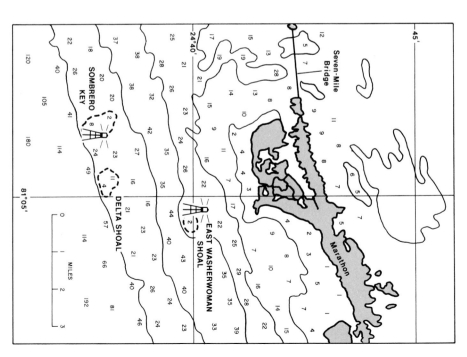

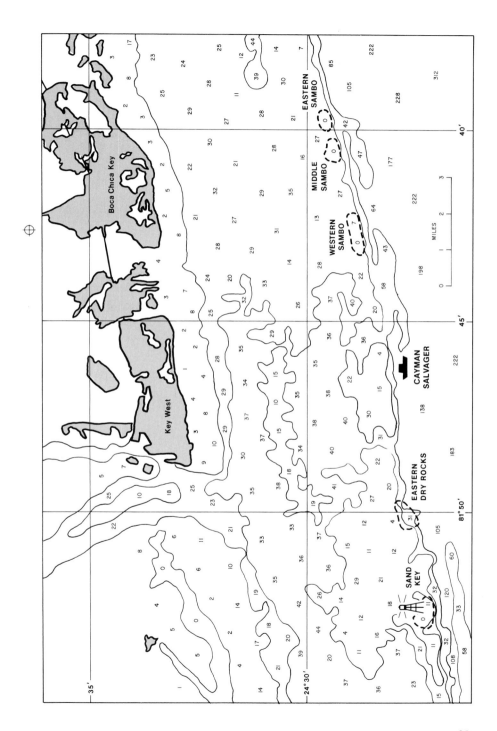

Key West

The diver willing to travel all the way to the end of the Keys will find he can mix the flavor of historic Key West with excellent diving opportunities.

Topped by a one hundred foot light tower, Sand Key is one of the most popular sites in the Key West area. It is similar to many of the other Keys' reefs, offering snorkeling depths and deep-water scuba depths. The striking coral formations offer unusual backgrounds for photography and a haven for large and small sea life. Eastern Dry Rocks is a couple of miles east.

The Sambo's, ranging from 7 to 10 miles SE of Key West, include Western, Middle and Eastern Sambo. You could dive these reefs for days and never finish exploring them. The 65-foot shrimp boat, *Captain Allen,* sits on Middle Sambo above water and aids in locating the reefs. You're sure to find a few big conch shells out here.

One of the best wreck dives in the Lower Keys is on the destroyer *Alexander,* sunk about 1942 in 35 feet of water. It is broken into two large pieces and can be seen partly exposed above water, about a 10 mile run NW of Key West. (Not shown on chart.) One of the newest is the *Cayman Salvager* wreck. It's a 180-foot buoy tender resting in 90 feet of water on the edge of the Gulf Stream.

Naples

The best scuba sites around Naples are found on two artificial reefs south of the city off the coast of Marco Island. The first reef, called Reef One, is

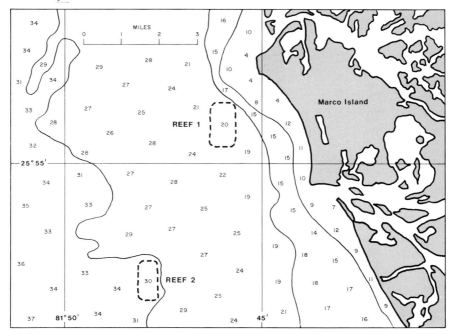

less than two miles from Marco Island and is made up of old auto tires piled a few feet high. Depths over this reef average about 20 feet. The second reef (Reef Two) is about five miles southwest of Marco and lies in 30 feet of water. It's higher than the first reef and is made up of concrete, steel, a sunken barge and old trucks.

Unfortunately for the spearfisherman, spearing is not allowed in Collier County. Some big grouper and large snapper schools are found on the reefs. Divers have also reported seeing huge tarpon, amberjacks, thick schools of snook, jewfish and barracuda. Tropical fish collectors have picked up some nice angelfish and butterflyfish specimens.

Boatless scuba divers and snorkelers will be interested in checking out Doctor's Pass just north of the city and Watt's Reef off Vanderbilt Beach. You'll see tropicals, schools of grunt, seahorses, sponges and shells.

Fort Myers

Sanibel Island is located about 15 miles SW of Fort Myers and is accessible by car. For years Sanibel has been known as a sheller's paradise, and for this reason divers from all over the state are drawn to the calm, warm waters surrounding the island to hunt for sea shells. There is no one single spot that rates above the others — anywhere around the island is a likely spot so put in where it's most convenient for you.

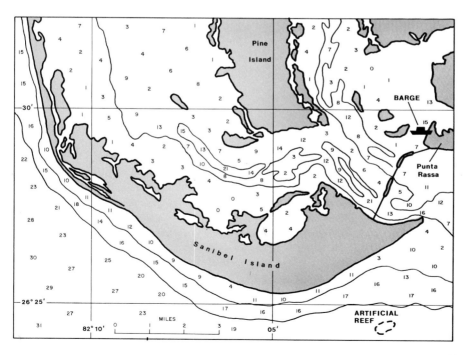

There's an inshore barge wreck about 100 yards off Punta Rassa Marina. It is 140 feet long and lying on its side in 15 feet of water. Don't be surprised if you see a jewfish under it, and in fact, a few divers have reported seeing a couple of dolphin pass by. Strong tidal currents are common over the wreck.

If the barge isn't exciting enough for you, sign up for a trip out to the *Bayronto*, also called the Boca Grande Wreck. It's 35 miles west of Ft. Myers but well worth the ride. The *Bayronto* is a 420-foot freighter which sank in 1919 with a cargo of grain. It lies in 100 feet of water in an upside-down position and serves as an artificial reef for thousands of fish. Great schools of snook, big jewfish, cobia, tarpon and amberjack are just a sampling of the species that frequent the wreck. Guided trips with large Loran-equipped boats are available in town. (Not shown on chart.)

Sarasota

There are four good scuba diving reefs near Sarasota ranging from 10 to 14 miles offshore from Crescent Beach. The local names for each of the reefs were derived from a distinctive feature. Bonita Bed is noted for its unusual bonita population. Turtle reef has a large live-in turtle on it. Coral Head Reef is crowned by a seven-foot high coral formation. And Horseshoe Reef was named for its shape. They all hold an impressive fish population and you can always pick up a few lobster on them.

South of Crescent Beach is the popular Point-of-Rocks area which will keep snorkelers busy for hours studying the sea life, looking for shells and maybe even finding a couple of stone crabs.

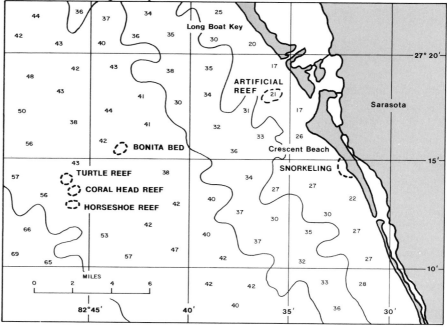

Bradenton

A sunken barge, known locally as the "Sugar Barge", can be reached by swimming less than 100 yards offshore from Trader Jack's Restaurant, just north of the Cortez Bridge in Bradenton Beach. The 200-foot ship sank in 20 feet of water with the uppermost part breaking the surface. It's a popular spot for scuba checkout dives and an easy swim for snorkelers.

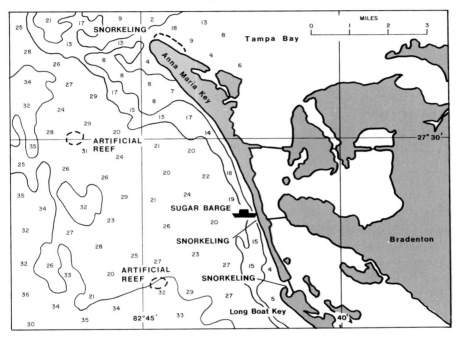

At the tip of Anna Maria Key you'll find interesting snorkeling for shells but use caution during times of active currents.

Other good snorkeling spots are located around the rocks at Bradenton Beach and along the north end of Long Boat Key.

Tampa

The greater Tampa area has long been the center of diving activity for the Gulf Coast. Diving guides with large, fast boats, fully-equipped to reach distant offshore sites can be found in Tampa, St. Petersburg, Clearwater and Madeira Beach.

The goal of many novice scuba divers is to make a dive on the *Mexican Pride*. It's far, and it's deep, but it's an awesome sight and a fabulous dive.

The "Pride" wreck is a 400-foot Liberty Ship sunk around the late 60's. It lies about 40 miles west of the Tampa Bay entrance in 130 feet of water, top decks starting at 80 feet. Everything is bigger out here: the grouper, red

43

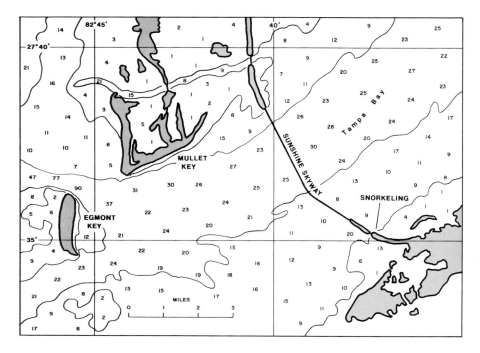

snapper, cobia, amberjack, barracuda and the jewfish. Generally clear water offers great photo opportunities.

Interesting ledge diving in 40 to 50 foot depths is found at South Jack Hole, located about 5 miles south of the last whistler buoy out of the Tampa channel. Both the spearfisherman and the tropical fish collector will have plenty to choose from here.

Another good area lies 18 to 25 miles due west of John's Pass near Madeira Beach. Rocks and ledges found in 55-60 foot depths are alive with lobster, grouper and hog snapper. Also there is good shelling especially for cowries and conchs.

Snorkeling is good at Fort Desoto Park on Mullet Key. Clams, starfish, sand dollars and mollusks are found in 4 to 6 foot depths. With a boat you can try snorkel or shallow scuba diving at Egmont Key about a mile SW of Mullet Key. It's a good site for exploring. Another skin diver's spot, and a very accessible one, is around the rocks at the south end of the Skyway Bridge. Use caution during heavy current activity in these areas.

Two fairly recent shipwrecks are now a part of the greater Tampa diving scene. More than 20 miles west of Clearwater Pass lies the *Blackthorn* in 80 feet of water. It was a coast guard ship originally sunk by a freighter in Tampa Bay, refloated and resunk.

Another popular wreck is the 65-foot *Gunsmoke*. This was a shrimp boat used by smugglers. It's also in 80-foot depths over 20 miles west of Egmont Key. Both wrecks are excellent dives.

44

Crystal River

Crystal River is a mecca for fresh-water divers — snorkel and scuba — and one of the most popular inland sites in the state.

The head of the river is a large area, appearing more like a lake, and containing several islands and springs. The greatest attraction is around King Spring, a few yards south of Banana Island. The center of the spring is surrounded by 20-25 foot cliffs; a cave at the bottom drops straight down to nearly 60 feet. It's a good spot for beginning cave divers. All around King Spring are shallow-water areas filled with aquatic plants and plenty of fish — both fresh and salt water species. Large schools of mangrove snapper and mullet are usually around, plus needlefish, sheepshead, gar and even the mighty tarpon. During the winter months the enormous, docile manatees, or sea cows, venture up the river to feed around the spring areas.

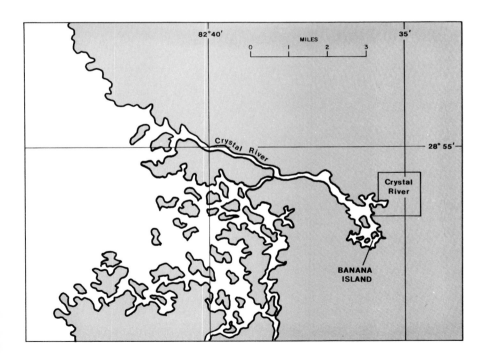

A few yards west of King Spring is the Grand Canyon area. The canyon runs for 35 feet between sheer rock walls that plunge to 25 feet. On the other side of King Spring are a few other springs in 20 foot depths.

The head of Crystal River is located within the town of Crystal River making it easy to find. Diving services are available on the river.

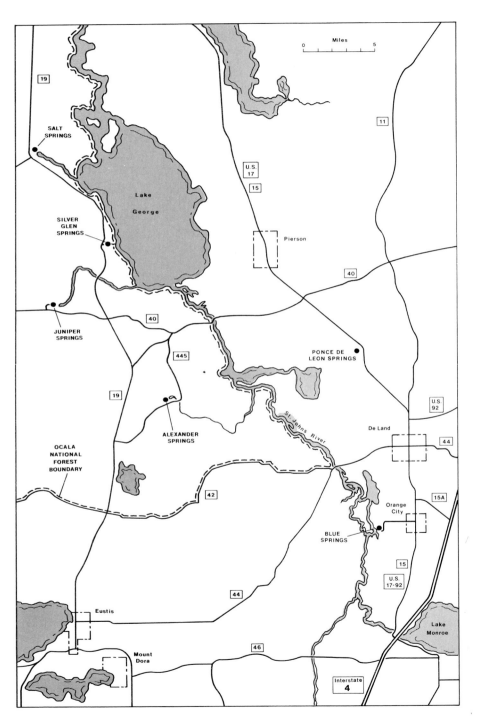

Miles
0   5

19

SALT
SPRINGS

11

U.S.
17

15

Lake
George

Pierson

SILVER
GLEN
SPRINGS

40

40

JUNIPER
SPRINGS

445

PONCE DE
LEON SPRINGS

19

U.S.
92

St. Johns River

De Land

44

ALEXANDER
SPRINGS

OCALA
NATIONAL
FOREST
BOUNDARY

15A

42

Orange
City

BLUE
SPRINGS

44

15

U.S.
17-92

Eustis

Lake
Monroe

Mount
Dora

46

Interstate
4

Ocala National Forest

There are four major spring areas within Ocala: Juniper, Salt, Silver Glen and Alexander. They all have recreational areas built around them and require entrance fees. Signs are located throughout the forest, directing you to the sites.

Alexander Springs is the most popular skin diving site in the area. Snorkelers will enjoy fishwatching in the large area around the spring, often sighting big bass, schools of shell crackers, bream, blue gills, and an occasional alligator gar. Scuba divers have an opportunity to check themselves out for fresh-water diving in the large cavern at the head of the spring. The hole is about 30 feet across and 30 feet deep with a small 10-foot cave at the bottom. Temperature is a steady 72°-73°F. There's a nice spot across from the swimming area for underwater photography. Scuba certification is required at the park entrance.

Silver Glen Springs is located north of Alexander. The spring water flows out of a boil at the bottom of a 30-foot vertical cavern and merges with Lake George a half mile away. The run is usually filled with schooling mullet, panfish and bass. You can snorkel around the boil and down the run but scuba diving is not allowed.

Juniper and Salt Springs have smaller head spring areas but they have interesting snorkeling down the runs.

Blue Springs — Orange City

Blue Springs is one of the few fresh-water sites in East Central Florida and serves many divers in the Daytona Beach and Orlando areas. It is located in a state recreation area just 2½ miles west of Orange City. Because of several diving accidents that have occurred in the spring, the park requires that divers have proof of certification, a tank pressure gauge, a light, knife, watch and depth gauge.

The spring area is picturesque and well preserved. Many arrowheads and other artifacts have been found along the run.

This spring is the second largest single spring in the state, dispersing 160 cubic feet of water a second at a constant 72°F. Visibilities reach 100 feet. A wide entrance to a vertical cave starts at 10 feet and ends 125 feet down at the boil. Another passage extends upwards from the boil to about 65 feet.

The manatees move into the spring run from the St. Johns River in the fall, and since they are an endangered species, a section of the run is designated as a manatee refuge area.

High Springs

Blue Springs, near the town of High Springs, is a scenic area, both underwater and above the surface. At the headspring is a large basin with 25-foot depths surrounded by dramatic vertical rock formations and swaying plant life. The spring run to the Santa Fe River is good for fishwatching and fossil hunt-

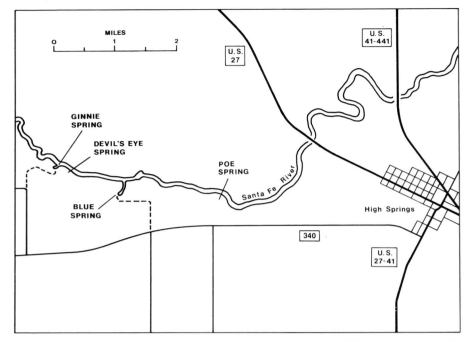

ing. After your run you can return to the headspring via a 1500-foot boardwalk that follows the length of the spring. Blue Springs is commercially operated and charges an admission fee. Scuba is not allowed.

To get to Blue Springs, from High Springs, turn west onto SR 340 from U.S. 27-41. About 4.2 miles down SR 340 you'll find a Blue Springs sign. Take a right down the wide dirt road and follow it until you come to the entrance gate.

Half the adventure of diving some of the springs is trying to find them. Ginnie is such a spring.

From the Blue Springs sign on SR 340, head west for two miles and take a right immediately after passing under the power lines. Travel down the wide dirt road for 1.1 miles and you are at the entrance to Ginnie Springs. This area is also a commercial operation and has many facilities for the diver such as a store, camping facilities, air station, etc.

At Ginnie's headspring, about 20 feet below the surface, is a cave entrance which permits entry into a large cavity called the "Ballroom." This room gently slopes downward to about 60 feet. At the end of the room are two tunnels that extend deep underground and should be avoided by novice cave divers. Other springs in this area include Devil's Eye and Poe.

Fort White

From Fort White, go 2 miles north on Rte. 47, then turn left on SR 238 and drive 4 miles to the Ichetucknee Springs State Park entrance.

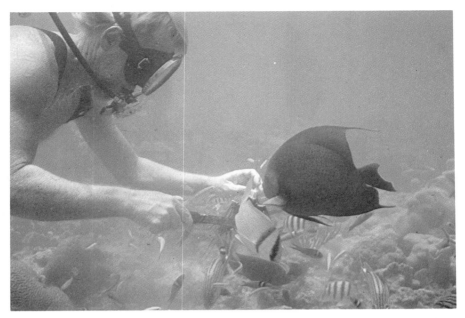

Divers are not strangers to angelfish and other reef fish, which are often brazen, especially when they are offered bits of sea urchin—a delicacy most fish are denied because of the urchin's sharp spines.

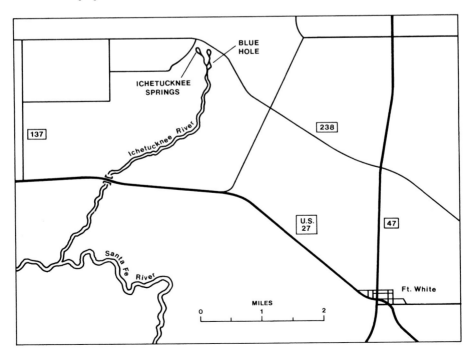

The main spring flows out of a 17-foot basin to form the Ichetucknee River. The clear, beautiful river run is frequented by many snorkelers who enjoy drift-diving with the current. There are quite a few fish, green turtles, and striking underwater scenery to see. Depths range from waist-deep to 12-15 feet. Once you start the run, you have committed yourself to a 3½ mile trip until you reach the bridge on U.S. 27. There's a large area here where you can leave a car or catch a bus back to the state park. The long exposure to the cool spring water necessitates the use of wet suits.

Also in the state park is Blue Hole Spring where scuba diving is allowed. It's accessible by taking the pathway a few yards past the park entrance. The opening to a vertical cave starts at 10 feet, drops down to 37 feet, then widens and ends at 55 feet.

Branford

The snorkeler may not find Little River Spring very interesting, but for scuba divers it's a first-rate cave dive.

From Branford center, travel three miles north on Rte. 129. Take a left on SR 248 and go 1.7 miles to the dirt road bearing left. The spring is at the end of the road.

There isn't much of a run at Little River — the Suwannee River can be seen from the head of the spring. About 15 feet below the surface of the headspring is a wide cave entrance that drops to 60-80 feet. From here experienced cave divers will pick up a corridor which snakes down to 110 feet. Farther

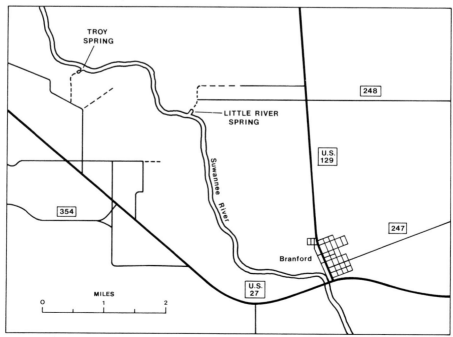

on through, the tunnel will take you to a passage on the right which allows entry into the Terminal Room, named for its resemblance to a railroad switching station. Returning to the main corridor will lead you to the Florida Room, the largest room ever discovered in this state.

Several disasters have occurred to novice scuba divers at Little River Spring. Do not attempt it unless you're thoroughly trained in cave diving procedures.

Another good spot around the Branford area is Troy Spring. From Branford, travel west on Rte. 27. After four miles you'll pass SR 354, continue straight for another ¾ mile until you come to the next paved road on the right. After 1.2 miles down this road you'll find a narrow dirt road on the right just in front of two mobile homes. This road will take you to the spring ½ mile away.

The large basin at Troy plunges to 80-foot depths providing interesting cliff formations. There is a short spring run to the Suwannee River. At the end of the run lies the remains of a confederate gunboat in only a few feet of water.

Panama City

Talk to a Panama City diver and the conversation invariably turns to the "Mica". The *Empire Mica* is a 400-foot tanker that met the same fate as dozens of other ships during the daring U-boat attacks along the Florida coast in 1942. The ship received a direct torpedo hit that virtually split the craft in two and

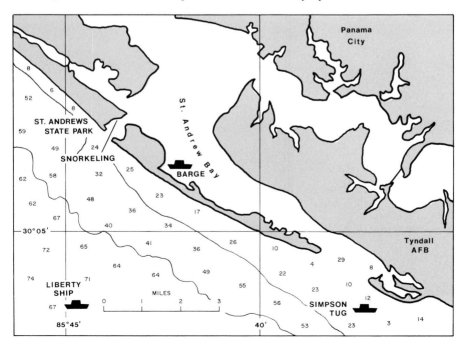

sent it to the bottom in 115 feet of water. Its location is about 24 miles south of Cape San Blas.

The wreck of the *Empire Mica* rates as one of the top dives off the Panhandle coast. (Not shown on chart.)

Other deep-water dives include the wrecks *Grey Ghost* and the *Chicasaw* sunk as part of an artificial reef program.

A much closer wreck can be found about half a mile off the coast near Tyndall A.F.B. It's the tugboat, *E. E. Simpson*, which sank in 1936 in about 12 feet of water.

A U.S. Navy platform (not the one seen from shore) is a good spot to pick up a nice black or warsaw grouper. It is located about 13 miles south of Panama City in 100 feet of water. Before you dive it, first check with authorities to learn if it's currently permissible to dive the site. (Not shown on chart.)

Snorkelers and novice scuba divers will like the pass at St. Andrews State Park. Depths here range from inches to 30 feet and you will find schools of jack crevalle, mullet, stone crabs and tropicals.

For the novice wreck diver, there's a sunken barge just offshore in St. Andrew's Bay. For a more advanced wreck dive, a Liberty Ship can be found several miles offshore in 70 feet of water.

Pensacola

Pensacola is noted for its excellent artificial reef diving. Just a few miles off Pensacola Beach you'll find a large Liberty ship, several barges and an airplane

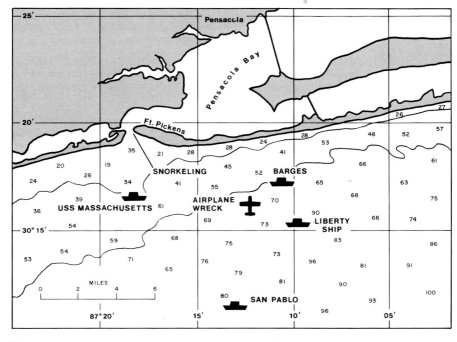

Underwater Florida provides a variety of tropical fish for saltwater aquarium enthusiasts. Some of the most beautiful and prized are the angelfish, including the two species pictured—gray angelfish (top), and the French angelfish.

wreck. Check-out diving is good on the battleship "Massachusetts" in shallow water off Ft. Pickens.

The hottest spot in the area is the wreck of the *San Pablo,* a Russian freighter believed to have gone down during WWII in 80 feet of water. It's broken up now but there are big sections that attract schools of spearing fish. Along with a choice of grouper, snapper and spadefish, you can pick up a few flounder. Tropical fish collectors are content with choosing from a variety of drum, angelfish, damselfish and cardinals. The wreck is about nine miles south of Pensacola Beach.

Many divers feel it's worth the 20-mile trip from Navarre to dive the Timber Hole, a rocky formation with plenty of holes and ledges to draw a large fish population. Big lobster can be gathered here and the amberjack, snapper and grouper abound. It's an advanced diver site with the bottom averaging about 110 feet deep. (Not shown on chart.)

For snorkeling or scuba check out, try the pass off Ft. Pickens in the Gulf Islands National Seashore for off-the-beach diving into 20-foot depths. You'll find tropicals and some nice shells including murex, tulips and whelks.

Shipwrecks

Nobody knows exactly how many ships have been lost off the coast of Florida since the beginning of the recorded history, but current estimates reach as high as 4000.

It's very possible. For centuries, ships from many nations have sailed these waters. The Spanish were the first influence in the New World. Many of their ships, often treasure-laden, crashed on the shallow reefs and shoals as they journeyed back to Spain. Later the French, British and Americans became active in Florida expeditions and their ships, too, met similar fates. Early sailings were often hampered by bad weather, hostile acts or inadequate navigational aids.

Many of the treasure-bearing ships were salvaged or partially salvaged quickly after their destruction. Others have only recently been discovered and many, many others have yet to be found. The following map illustrates a few of the general locations where wealthy ships have been lost.

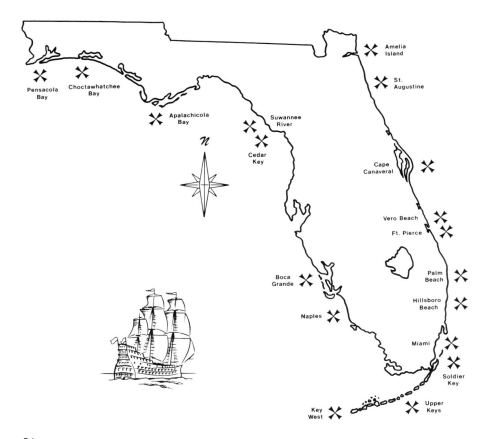

Treasure Sites

Amelia Island   A favorite haunt of pirates and the site of many shipwrecks on the hazardous shoals near the island.

St. Augustine   Two Spanish ships sank in 1572 and another wrecked in 1626 on the shallows off the inlet. Thousands of coins were aboard both ships. Many other British, Spanish and American ships were lost on the treacherous St. Augustine sand bars.

Cape Canaveral   Another area rich with lost ships, new and old. Among them, the *San Nicolas* wrecked south of the cape in 1551 with treasure aboard.

Vero Beach   Ten ships of the 1715 silver fleet are scattered in this area from Sebastian Inlet to Ft. Pierce. Nearly $30 million in gold, silver and jewels has been recovered by the Real Eight Co. and there is more to be found. At press time, the galleon *San Roman* was discovered along with $300,000 of treasure, but the treasure hunters believe they are close to finding six boxes of gold coins, worth an estimated $60 million.

Ft. Pierce   The British barkentine, *Reformation,* sank four miles south of the St. Lucie Inlet with Spanish coins aboard. A skin diver found thousands of dollars in U.S. Army payroll money just off Pepper Park. Other coins have been found on the beach ½ mile south of the Ft. Pierce Inlet.

Palm Beach   Three Spanish ships sank off Palm Beach in a 1554 hurricane with gold and silver aboard. Part of a $7 million treasure was recovered from the Spanish galleon *Santa Margarita* resting in these waters.

Hillsboro Beach   Skin divers have found silver coins off Hillsboro Inlet believed to belong to a Spanish ship.

Miami   The galleon *Santa Margarita* (not the same as above) was lost in Biscayne Bay in 1595 near the Cutler area. Several million is assumed to be aboard. Spanish coins have been found in this area.

Soldier Key   A British Frigate went down in 1829 with $2 million on board.

Upper Keys   Millions in treasure have been salvaged from countless wrecks on the reefs off the Keys with many ships still unaccounted. The most notable salvage effort took place on the wrecks of the 1733 fleet scattered along the Upper Keys.

Key West   Recent discoveries have pinpointed wrecks of the incredibly rich 1622 fleet in waters west of Key West. In 1985, the *Nuestra Señora de Atocha* was discovered along with an estimated $300-$400 million in silver and gold.

Naples   Spanish gold coins have been found washed up on Naples beaches.

Boca Grande   Gasparilla Island, southwest of Punta Gorda, was the camp of the noted pirate, José Gaspar. Coins have been found around the Boca Grande Channel, possibly belonging to the pirate's flagship sunk by U.S. ships. $10 million is estimated to have been aboard.

Cedar Key Spanish money was found on the seaward shore of Cedar Key, supporting the theory of a nearby sunken treasure ship.

Suwannee River An American schooner supposedly carrying part of the purchase price for the territory of Florida sank in 1820 at the mouth of the Suwannee River. Some coins have been found.

Port St. Joe In the west pass of Apalachicola Bay, a pirate frigate sank with $5 million in silver on board.

Ft. Walton Beach Strong rumors that the pirate, Billy Bowlegs burned his ship, the *Mysterio*, in the Choctawhatchee Bay when chased by the British. Possibly $4 million on board at the time.

What appears to be nothing more than a clump of corroded rocks is actually part of the vast treasure recovered off Vero Beach from the famous 1715 silver fleet wrecks. These once-gleaming coins became encrusted and fused together after remaining under the sea for over 250 years.

Photo courtesy Florida Department of Commerce

Two excellent examples of Spanish gold doubloons ("Pieces of Eight") are displayed here after they have been thoroughly cleaned. Although these pieces are almost perfectly round, many Spanish gold and silver coins were stamped in a variety of odd shapes.

Pensacola   In a 1559 hurricane, six Spanish ships went down in Pensacola Bay with a cargo of silver aboard. A storm sank the treasure-laden *Volador II* in 1815 in this area. In one storm in 1778, 14 ships were sunk at Pensacola.

This is only a sampling of the riches that lie beneath the water along the coast of Florida. With the increasing popularity of skin diving, these and many others are bound to be discovered in the future.

The state of Florida has a firm hand on salvage attempts within its waters. Anyone interested in exploring or salvaging a wreck area must be approved by the state, pay a fee and post bond.

Artifacts and Fossils

Treasure doesn't have to glisten like a gold doubloon or a precious stone to be considered treasure. To an archeologist, a wealthy find may take the form of a piece of old Indian pottery, and a rare fossilized bone may be priceless to a paleontologist. What has all this to do with diving? Many major artifact and fossil finds were made in the springs and rivers of Florida through skin diving, either by scientists using scuba as a tool in their searches or by sport divers who often work in cooperation with interested organizations.

A majority of the fossils found in this state date back to the Pleistocene Period which existed nearly one million years ago. A few rare finds have been estimated at 50 million years old. Divers have uncovered well-preserved fossils of Mammoths, Mastodons, Saber-toothed Tigers, camels and even parts of a giant carnivorous bird.

The Spanish were the first major influence in Florida as they explored and eventually colonized the state during the 16th and 17th centuries. After America won its independence, the British poured into the state until England returned Florida back to Spain. The Seminole Indians were very active during the early 19th Century and, of course, the Civil War brought armies of soldiers to many of the forts in the state. Today, divers are finding arrowheads, pottery, tools, utensils, weapons and old bottles used by these past residents of the state. Tangible evidence of Florida's colorful past is often found in the sand and mud beneath the water.

NOTE: Divers should be aware of the Florida law which states that all artifacts, fossils or objects having historical or archaeological value found on state-owned submersed land are the property of the state.

Air Stations

The following map shows the general locations of nearly every air station in the state. Along with air service, most of the sites contain fully-equipped dive shops offering equipment sales and rentals, scuba instruction, equipment repair and guide services.

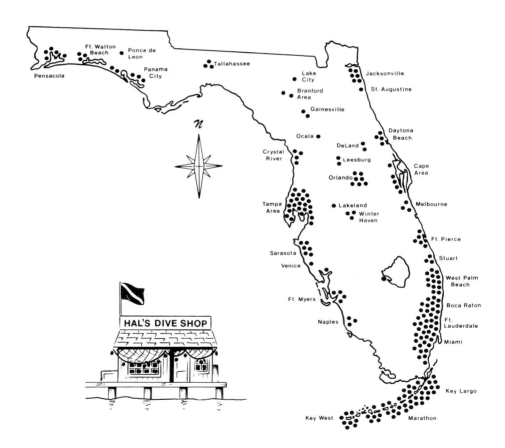

Sharks

The shark has been the center of a considerable amount of attention in recent years. Writers and film-makers find the shark a fascinating subject for exciting, dramatic (often traumatic) stories. In the process they have created a few misconceptions about the creature.

Visiting divers often ask: "What are the odds of a shark attacking a skin diver in Florida's water?" The answer may be found in these facts.

There are over 250 species of sharks in the oceans of the world with about 40 of them known to have entered the waters of Florida. Of these 40, 12 species are considered dangerous to man (a dangerous shark is one that has attacked man on at least one occasion). Two of the 12, the mako and the great white, are predominantly pelagic, or open water sharks. Two others, the sand shark and the nurse shark have a very low danger rating. Those of most concern to swimmers or divers are the members of the hammerhead family (four species), the tiger shark, the large black tip, the bull and the lemon shark.

Of course, for a shark attack to take place, there must be a shark in the diver's area. Many very active divers have never seen a shark, much less a dangerous one. Florida is not known for supporting a very high shark population.

Even if a dangerous shark spots a diver, the shark will not indiscriminately attack the diver on sight. In fact, the diver is not as appealing to a shark as a swimmer thrashing on the surface or a surfer dangling his limbs from a surfboard. Also, divers have the advantage of being able to sight the shark and take necessary steps before the creature makes a decision. Diving in groups also tends to disinterest sharks.

Of the extremely few attacks that have occurred to divers, most were attributed to divers who actually provoked a shark or teased the animal with a freshly-speared fish.

The odds of a swimmer being attacked in these waters have been calculated somewhere around five million to one—a diver's odds are even better.

The chances of your being the victim of a shark attack may be very low but just about everybody agrees that sharks are indeed very unpredictable. If a shark is sighted, even one considered harmless, the safest action for a snorkeler to take is to head back for the beach or boat as calmly and deliberately as possible, keeping an eye on the shark's whereabouts. Scuba divers are recommended to remain on the bottom with their backs to a rock or other object and keep the shark in view until it leaves. Don't try to spear it with a conventional spear gun.

In the final analysis, don't let fear of sharks be your reason for not diving in Florida.

The sluggish nurse shark frequents shallow waters around reefs. Though not normally a threat to divers, the nurse shark can inflict a painful bite if threatened or molested.

Hazardous Marine Life

Within the sea there are several species of life that pose a threat of injury to the skin diver. Many divers new to the sea are either completely unaware of these hazards or imagine the ocean to be infested with animals ready to bite, sting, cut, stab or poison him the instant he enters the water.

Florida does have its share of dangerous marine animals, but fortunately they are less abundant than they are in other seas of the world. A description of species capable of seriously injuring the Florida skin diver follows.

Barracuda

There are very few Florida divers who aren't familiar with members of the *Sphyraena* clan — better known as the barracuda family. The favorite pastime of these fish seems to be an insatiable desire to stalk skin divers. They will appear out of nowhere, follow the diver for awhile, then disappear as quickly as they appeared. Actually it's all part of their act. Barracuda bites are almost as rare as mermaid sightings. A few incidents have occurred, though, primarily in murky water when the 'cuda mistook a shiny object on a swimmer for a small baitfish.

Basically, there are two types of barracuda found in Florida. The smaller varieties are about a foot or two long and sport predominantly silver, torpedo-shaped bodies. The larger 'cudas, or the great barracuda, have the same general shape but magnified to 5 feet or more. The major difference is in the camouflaging pattern of dark bars running down the sides and black blotches near the tails. The great barracuda is not as silvery as the smaller barracuda; instead it is colored a greenish-gray on top with a white belly.

Barracudas are not aggressive to divers but neither are they afraid. Trying to scare a 'cuda away usually results in a display of his razor-sharp teeth. It's not advisable to provoke the creature, and if you cross paths with a big one — let him have the right-of-way.

Stingrays

Stingrays are fairly common throughout Florida. They are bottom dwellers, often seen resting partly exposed in the sand. They have flat bodies with very large wing-like pectoral fins which give them roughly a diamond

The irregular leafy body of the scorpionfish provides excellent camouflage as it passively waits for prey to pass by, and it can inflict a painful wound to an unwary diver who accidentally steps on the venomous spiny fin.

Fire coral are not true corals, but are a frequent component of the reef. Brushing against fire coral will cause a burning sensation and reddening of the skin.

61

shape. All stingrays have long slender tails affixed with a movable spine about the size of a nail. If stepped on, the ray will whip its tail, sending the venomous spine into its victim's flesh.

Most often the stingray will scatter at the presence of a diver. Shuffling the sand with swim fins will also scare them off. Stingrays vary in size from the small, one-foot yellow ray to the six-foot wide eagle rays.

Stingray wounds will cause considerable pain and swelling. Treat an inflicted area by first cleaning with cold water, then soaking in hot water for about half an hour.

Manta Rays

The giant manta ray, or devil ray, looks like it was made to gobble up skin divers. On the contrary, it is a non-aggressive, non-stinging animal and does not pose a serious threat to divers. It can startle a diver though, if he should spot one of these huge rays soaring overhead. They can have an extraordinary "wing-span" of 20 feet and weigh as much as 3500 pounds. Boaters sighting the manta ray's fins cutting the water often mistake them for sharks or porpoises.

Moray Eel

The slippery, slithering moray eels make their homes under rocks, in coral holes and crevices, and in shipwrecks. Spotted morays grow to about 3 feet and the more common green moray can reach an impressive 6 feet in length. They have small, sharp teeth — which they like to show off to divers — set in a head too small for their thick, snake-like bodies. They seldom leave their lairs and won't attack a diver unless threatened. They are often seen partly out of their holes but many prefer complete privacy, so avoid sticking your hands in places that could possibly be a moray's home. If you are bitten by a moray, control the bleeding, wash the area thoroughly and clean with a disinfectant. They're not venomous creatures but a bite could cause infection.

Some divers have found that they could hand-feed moray eels, but it might be best to save the snacks for the more docile reef fish.

Scorpionfish

If the queen angelfish is the "beauty", then the scorpionfish must be the "beast." These unattractive creatures usually average about a foot in length, have a bulldog face and a rough, warty skin which enables them to blend well with the terrain, usually rocky reef areas.

This fish's advantage is a diver's disadvantage if he fails to see through the camouflage and accidentally steps on the scorpion's dorsal fin. The Atlantic scorpionfish isn't as deadly as the Pacific varieties but contact with the venomous spiny fin will cause considerable pain and swelling.

Treatment of a scorpionfish wound is similar to that of a snake bite. Wash the inflicted area with cold water and cut across the puncture marks to suck out the venom. Soak in hot water, alternating with cold water to keep the swelling down. Seek prompt medical attention.

Portuguese Man-Of-War

The tropical Portuguese Man-Of-War is not a single animal but a massive colony of tiny hydroids. These microscopic animals are suspended from the surface of the water, or just below the surface, by a pinkish-blue gas-filled float, usually measuring from several inches to a foot long. Below the float trail dozens of coiled tentacles extending downward to 50 feet or longer. The long strands contain millions of stinging cells used to immobilize and capture fish swimming through the stinging threads.

They have the same effect upon unwary swimmers and divers who accidentally come in contact with them. The cells discharge a venom onto the skin which immediately produces an intense pain.

Treat a Man-Of-War sting by removing the clinging tentacles with a towel and clean the wound with diluted ammonia, vinegar or rubbing alcohol. If the injury is extreme seek immediate medical attention.

Sea Urchins

Sea urchins are small invertebrates belonging to the starfish family. They carry an arsenal of spines jutting out in all directions giving them a strong resemblance to a pin cushion. If stepped on, their sharp brittle spines will penetrate, and often break off into the skin. To treat an urchin wound, pull out all exposed pieces; those imbedded deep within the skin will dissolve within a few days. Clean the affected area, apply an antiseptic and dress the wound.

Fire Coral

While diving on coral reefs, keep an eye open for fire coral mixed with the other formations. There are two basic types: one (branching fire coral) looks like a miniature staghorn coral with tiny branches, the other is a leafy type (plate fire coral) resembling folds in a drape. They aren't true stony corals and appear much smoother than the porous polyp corals. They can be recognized by their distinctive mustard color.

Brushing against fire coral will cause a burning sensation and a reddening of the skin. Rinse an affected area with a diluted ammonia solution and wash with soap and water.

Along with the species described here, there are lesser hazards that exist in the way of small hydroids, anemones, jellyfish, bristleworms, etc. A good rule to remember is don't touch anything in the sea unless you know what it is and are certain it can't harm you.

Florida Diving Laws

Anyone intending to dive in the waters surrounding Florida should be aware of the many laws governing certain aspects of sport diving, primarily lobstering and spearfishing. Divers unaware of these laws expose themselves to possible fines. Anyone who fishes Florida's salt waters must possess a valid **Florida salt water fishing license.** Bridge and surf fishermen who are Florida residents are exempt but it is necessary for anyone who spearfishes or takes sea life by any other method, including taking lobster by hand.

The following information will answer many of the questions concerning the state's diving laws, but it should only be used as a guideline. Laws can be added or changed quickly and *it's the diver's responsibility* to keep himself informed on the latest legal developments.

Crawfish Laws

Remember these legal points regarding the taking of Florida's spiny lobster (crawfish):

- Lobster season lasts eight months, from August through March. No lobster can be taken from April 1st through the end of July. *
- You cannot take egg-carrying females *anytime*. They can be identified by the large cluster of bright-orange eggs carried under the tail.
- The limit is 6 lobster per person or 24 to a boat.
- Legal size is at least 3 inches across the carapace (upper shell). Divers must possess a special measuring gauge available at many dive shops.
- Lobster can only be taken by hand. You cannot spear, gig or net a crawfish.
- The tails cannot be removed until the catch is brought to shore.
- Commercial lobster traps must be left alone.

Spearfishing Laws

It's illegal to spearfish—
- within the boundaries of the John Pennekamp Coral Reef State Park.
- in Collier County (the Naples area).
- in Monroe County (the Keys) from Long Key north to the Dade County line (3 miles either side).
- within one mile of Route One from Long Key to Key West.
- within 100 yards of all public beaches, fishing piers, bridges with catwalks and jetties.
- in fresh water or for fresh-water fish in brackish water.
- ornamental reef fish or any gamefish, such as dolphin, sailfish, tarpon, etc.
- snook, striped bass, spiny lobster or stone crabs. **

Bag limits are the same as for hook-and-line fishing.

It's also illegal to
- take, injure or kill marine turtles, manta rays, porpoises and manatees.
- take coral or other specimens from the Coral Reef State Park or the Biscayne National Monument north of the state park.
- capture tropical fish with the use of drugs or poisons.

> All divers should display the traditional divers-down flag (red background with white diagonal stripe) while underwater and the international Alpha flag (half white, half blue) if divers are attached to the vessel.

Other diver-related laws may exist in individual counties. If you have any questions, contact the marine patrol office nearest you.

*Dates subject to annual change.
**One claw of the stone crab can be taken but the crab must be released alive. Legal size is a 2¾ in. forearm. Closed season—May 15 to Oct. 15.